50 Side Dishes to Elevate Any Meal Recipes for Home

By: Kelly Johnson

Table of Contents

- Garlic Roasted Potatoes
- Sautéed Spinach with Garlic
- Baked Macaroni and Cheese
- Grilled Asparagus with Lemon Zest
- Parmesan Roasted Brussels Sprouts
- Creamy Scalloped Potatoes
- Couscous with Roasted Vegetables
- Roasted Butternut Squash with Sage
- Balsamic Glazed Carrots
- Herb Butter Corn on the Cob
- Wild Rice Pilaf
- Cauliflower Mash
- Stuffed Bell Peppers
- Honey-Roasted Parsnips
- Mediterranean Quinoa Salad
- Cheesy Garlic Bread
- Broccoli with Lemon Butter
- Grilled Zucchini Ribbons
- Creamy Polenta with Parmesan
- Sautéed Mushrooms with Garlic
- Roasted Red Pepper Hummus
- Colcannon (Mashed Potatoes with Cabbage)
- Caprese Salad
- Grilled Sweet Potatoes
- Greek Orzo Salad
- Fried Plantains
- Herb-Roasted Root Vegetables
- Spinach and Artichoke Dip
- Zesty Lime Cilantro Rice
- Roasted Garlic Mashed Potatoes
- Creamed Corn with Bacon
- Grilled Eggplant with Herbs
- Dill Pickle Pasta Salad
- Tomato Basil Bruschetta
- Smashed Potatoes with Rosemary

- Sweet Potato Casserole
- Sesame Green Beans
- Three-Cheese Cauliflower Gratin
- Moroccan-Spiced Carrots
- Grilled Polenta Cakes
- Oven-Baked Parmesan Fries
- Sautéed Swiss Chard with Garlic
- Roasted Beets with Goat Cheese
- Maple-Glazed Acorn Squash
- Fennel and Apple Slaw
- Tomato Cucumber Salad
- Honey-Lime Roasted Carrots
- Pea and Mint Salad
- Crispy Kale Chips
- Wild Mushroom Risotto

Garlic Roasted Potatoes

Ingredients

- 2 pounds baby potatoes, halved
- 3 tablespoons olive oil
- 4 cloves garlic, minced
- 1 teaspoon dried thyme
- Salt and pepper to taste
- Fresh parsley for garnish

Instructions

1. **Preheat Oven:** Preheat your oven to 400°F (200°C) and line a baking sheet with parchment paper.
2. **Mix Ingredients:** In a large bowl, toss potatoes with olive oil, garlic, thyme, salt, and pepper until evenly coated.
3. **Roast Potatoes:** Spread the potatoes in a single layer on the baking sheet. Roast for 25-30 minutes until golden and crispy, stirring halfway.
4. **Garnish and Serve:** Garnish with fresh parsley before serving.

Sautéed Spinach with Garlic

Ingredients

- 1 pound fresh spinach, washed
- 3 tablespoons olive oil
- 4 cloves garlic, minced
- Salt and pepper to taste
- Juice of 1 lemon (optional)

Instructions

1. **Heat Oil:** In a large skillet, heat olive oil over medium heat. Add garlic and sauté for 1 minute until fragrant.
2. **Add Spinach:** Add spinach to the skillet and sauté for 3-5 minutes until wilted.
3. **Season and Serve:** Season with salt, pepper, and lemon juice if desired. Serve warm.

Baked Macaroni and Cheese

Ingredients

- 8 ounces elbow macaroni
- 2 cups sharp cheddar cheese, grated
- 1/2 cup grated Parmesan cheese
- 3 tablespoons butter
- 3 tablespoons all-purpose flour
- 2 cups milk
- Salt and pepper to taste
- Breadcrumbs for topping (optional)

Instructions

1. **Cook Pasta:** Preheat oven to 350°F (175°C). Cook macaroni according to package instructions, then drain.
2. **Make Cheese Sauce:** In a saucepan, melt butter over medium heat. Stir in flour, cooking for 1 minute. Gradually whisk in milk, stirring until thickened. Remove from heat and stir in cheddar and Parmesan until melted. Season with salt and pepper.
3. **Combine and Bake:** Combine cooked macaroni with cheese sauce. Transfer to a greased baking dish and top with breadcrumbs if desired. Bake for 20-25 minutes until bubbly and golden.
4. **Serve:** Serve hot as a comforting side or main dish.

Grilled Asparagus with Lemon Zest

Ingredients

- 1 pound asparagus, trimmed
- 2 tablespoons olive oil
- Salt and pepper to taste
- Zest of 1 lemon
- Juice of 1 lemon

Instructions

1. **Preheat Grill:** Preheat your grill to medium-high heat.
2. **Season Asparagus:** In a bowl, toss asparagus with olive oil, salt, and pepper.
3. **Grill Asparagus:** Grill asparagus for 5-7 minutes, turning occasionally, until tender and slightly charred.
4. **Add Lemon Zest:** Remove from the grill and drizzle with lemon juice and zest before serving.

Parmesan Roasted Brussels Sprouts

Ingredients

- 1 pound Brussels sprouts, halved
- 3 tablespoons olive oil
- 1/2 cup grated Parmesan cheese
- Salt and pepper to taste

Instructions

1. **Preheat Oven:** Preheat your oven to 400°F (200°C) and line a baking sheet with parchment paper.
2. **Season Brussels Sprouts:** In a bowl, toss Brussels sprouts with olive oil, Parmesan, salt, and pepper until evenly coated.
3. **Roast Brussels Sprouts:** Spread Brussels sprouts on the baking sheet in a single layer. Roast for 20-25 minutes until golden and crispy.
4. **Serve:** Serve warm as a delicious side dish.

Creamy Scalloped Potatoes

Ingredients

- 4 large russet potatoes, thinly sliced
- 2 cups heavy cream
- 1 cup sharp cheddar cheese, grated
- 2 tablespoons butter
- 2 cloves garlic, minced
- Salt and pepper to taste
- Fresh thyme for garnish (optional)

Instructions

1. **Preheat Oven:** Preheat your oven to 375°F (190°C) and grease a baking dish.
2. **Layer Potatoes:** In the baking dish, layer half of the potato slices, sprinkle with salt, pepper, and half of the garlic. Repeat with remaining potatoes and garlic.
3. **Add Cream:** Pour heavy cream evenly over the potatoes. Top with cheddar cheese and dot with butter.
4. **Bake:** Cover with foil and bake for 45 minutes. Remove foil and bake for an additional 15-20 minutes until golden and bubbly.
5. **Serve:** Garnish with fresh thyme if desired and serve hot.

Couscous with Roasted Vegetables

Ingredients

- 1 cup couscous
- 1 1/2 cups vegetable broth
- 2 cups mixed vegetables (bell peppers, zucchini, carrots)
- 2 tablespoons olive oil
- Salt and pepper to taste
- Fresh herbs for garnish (optional)

Instructions

1. **Preheat Oven:** Preheat your oven to 400°F (200°C) and line a baking sheet with parchment paper.
2. **Roast Vegetables:** Toss mixed vegetables with olive oil, salt, and pepper. Spread on the baking sheet and roast for 20-25 minutes until tender.
3. **Cook Couscous:** In a saucepan, bring vegetable broth to a boil. Stir in couscous, cover, and remove from heat. Let sit for 5 minutes, then fluff with a fork.
4. **Combine and Serve:** Mix roasted vegetables with couscous and garnish with fresh herbs if desired. Serve warm.

Enjoy these delicious and flavorful side dishes!

Roasted Butternut Squash with Sage

Ingredients

- 1 medium butternut squash, peeled and cubed
- 2 tablespoons olive oil
- 1 tablespoon fresh sage, chopped
- Salt and pepper to taste

Instructions

1. **Preheat the Oven:** Preheat your oven to 400°F (200°C) and line a baking sheet with parchment paper.
2. **Toss Squash:** In a bowl, toss the cubed butternut squash with olive oil, sage, salt, and pepper.
3. **Roast:** Spread the squash in an even layer on the baking sheet and roast for 25-30 minutes, stirring halfway through.
4. **Serve:** Serve hot, garnished with additional fresh sage if desired.

Balsamic Glazed Carrots

Ingredients

- 1 pound carrots, peeled and sliced
- 2 tablespoons balsamic vinegar
- 1 tablespoon honey
- 1 tablespoon olive oil
- Salt and pepper to taste

Instructions

1. **Preheat the Oven:** Preheat your oven to 400°F (200°C) and line a baking sheet with parchment paper.
2. **Toss Carrots:** In a bowl, mix carrots with olive oil, balsamic vinegar, honey, salt, and pepper.
3. **Roast:** Spread the carrots on the baking sheet and roast for 25-30 minutes, until tender and caramelized.
4. **Serve:** Serve immediately as a side dish.

Herb Butter Corn on the Cob

Ingredients

- 4 ears of corn, husked
- 2 tablespoons butter, melted
- 1 tablespoon fresh parsley, chopped
- 1 teaspoon fresh thyme, chopped
- Salt and pepper to taste

Instructions

1. **Boil or Grill Corn:** Boil the corn for 5-7 minutes or grill until lightly charred.
2. **Prepare Herb Butter:** In a small bowl, mix melted butter with parsley, thyme, salt, and pepper.
3. **Brush Corn:** Brush the hot corn with the herb butter mixture.
4. **Serve:** Serve immediately with extra herb butter if desired.

Wild Rice Pilaf

Ingredients

- 1 cup wild rice
- 2 cups vegetable broth
- 1/2 cup diced onions
- 1/4 cup dried cranberries
- 1/4 cup chopped walnuts
- 1 tablespoon olive oil
- Salt and pepper to taste

Instructions

1. **Cook Wild Rice:** In a saucepan, cook wild rice with vegetable broth according to package instructions.
2. **Sauté Onions:** In a skillet, heat olive oil and sauté onions until soft and translucent.
3. **Combine Ingredients:** Stir the cooked wild rice, sautéed onions, cranberries, and walnuts together. Season with salt and pepper.
4. **Serve:** Serve as a side dish or main dish for a flavorful meal.

Cauliflower Mash

Ingredients

- 1 head cauliflower, cut into florets
- 2 tablespoons butter
- 1/4 cup almond milk or cream
- Salt and pepper to taste

Instructions

1. **Steam Cauliflower:** Steam the cauliflower florets until tender, about 10 minutes.
2. **Blend or Mash:** Using a blender or potato masher, blend the cauliflower with butter, almond milk, salt, and pepper until smooth.
3. **Serve:** Serve hot as a low-carb alternative to mashed potatoes.

Stuffed Bell Peppers

Ingredients

- 4 large bell peppers, tops cut off and seeds removed
- 1 cup cooked quinoa or rice
- 1/2 cup black beans
- 1/2 cup corn
- 1/4 cup diced tomatoes
- 1 tablespoon olive oil
- 1 teaspoon cumin
- Salt and pepper to taste

Instructions

1. **Preheat the Oven:** Preheat your oven to 375°F (190°C).
2. **Prepare Filling:** In a bowl, mix the cooked quinoa, black beans, corn, diced tomatoes, olive oil, cumin, salt, and pepper.
3. **Stuff Peppers:** Stuff the mixture into the hollowed bell peppers.
4. **Bake:** Place the stuffed peppers in a baking dish and bake for 25-30 minutes.
5. **Serve:** Serve hot, garnished with fresh herbs or a drizzle of olive oil.

Honey-Roasted Parsnips

Ingredients

- 1 pound parsnips, peeled and sliced
- 2 tablespoons honey
- 2 tablespoons olive oil
- 1 teaspoon fresh thyme, chopped
- Salt and pepper to taste

Instructions

1. **Preheat the Oven:** Preheat your oven to 400°F (200°C) and line a baking sheet with parchment paper.
2. **Toss Parsnips:** In a bowl, toss parsnips with honey, olive oil, thyme, salt, and pepper.
3. **Roast:** Spread the parsnips on the baking sheet and roast for 25-30 minutes, stirring halfway through.
4. **Serve:** Serve as a sweet and savory side dish.

Enjoy making and sharing these delightful side dishes!

Mediterranean Quinoa Salad

Ingredients

- 1 cup cooked quinoa
- 1/2 cup cherry tomatoes, halved
- 1/4 cup cucumber, diced
- 1/4 cup Kalamata olives, pitted and sliced
- 1/4 cup feta cheese, crumbled
- 1 tablespoon olive oil
- 1 tablespoon lemon juice
- 1 teaspoon dried oregano
- Salt and pepper to taste

Instructions

1. **Prepare Ingredients:** Combine cooked quinoa, cherry tomatoes, cucumber, olives, and feta cheese in a large bowl.
2. **Make Dressing:** In a small bowl, whisk together olive oil, lemon juice, oregano, salt, and pepper.
3. **Mix and Serve:** Pour the dressing over the salad and toss to coat. Serve chilled or at room temperature.

Cheesy Garlic Bread

Ingredients

- 1 baguette, sliced lengthwise
- 1/4 cup butter, melted
- 2 cloves garlic, minced
- 1/2 cup shredded mozzarella
- 1/4 cup grated Parmesan
- 1 tablespoon fresh parsley, chopped

Instructions

1. **Preheat the Oven:** Preheat your oven to 375°F (190°C).
2. **Prepare Garlic Butter:** Mix melted butter with minced garlic and parsley.
3. **Assemble Bread:** Brush the garlic butter over the sliced baguette and top with mozzarella and Parmesan.
4. **Bake:** Place on a baking sheet and bake for 10-12 minutes, until cheese is bubbly and golden.
5. **Serve:** Slice and serve warm.

Broccoli with Lemon Butter

Ingredients

- 1 head of broccoli, cut into florets
- 2 tablespoons butter
- 1 tablespoon lemon juice
- 1 teaspoon lemon zest
- Salt and pepper to taste

Instructions

1. **Steam Broccoli:** Steam the broccoli florets until tender, about 5-7 minutes.
2. **Make Lemon Butter:** In a small pan, melt butter and stir in lemon juice, lemon zest, salt, and pepper.
3. **Toss Broccoli:** Pour the lemon butter over the steamed broccoli and toss to coat.
4. **Serve:** Serve as a refreshing side dish.

Grilled Zucchini Ribbons

Ingredients

- 2 large zucchinis
- 1 tablespoon olive oil
- 1 teaspoon balsamic vinegar
- Salt and pepper to taste
- Fresh basil, chopped (optional)

Instructions

1. **Prepare Zucchini:** Use a vegetable peeler to slice the zucchini into long, thin ribbons.
2. **Grill Zucchini:** Brush the zucchini ribbons with olive oil, season with salt and pepper, and grill for 1-2 minutes per side until lightly charred.
3. **Finish with Balsamic:** Drizzle with balsamic vinegar and garnish with fresh basil if desired.
4. **Serve:** Serve warm or at room temperature.

Creamy Polenta with Parmesan

Ingredients

- 1 cup polenta (cornmeal)
- 4 cups vegetable broth
- 1/4 cup grated Parmesan cheese
- 2 tablespoons butter
- Salt and pepper to taste

Instructions

1. **Cook Polenta:** In a saucepan, bring vegetable broth to a boil. Slowly whisk in the polenta, reduce heat to low, and cook, stirring frequently, until thickened (about 15-20 minutes).
2. **Add Cheese and Butter:** Stir in Parmesan cheese, butter, salt, and pepper.
3. **Serve:** Serve hot as a side dish, optionally topped with more cheese.

Sautéed Mushrooms with Garlic

Ingredients

- 2 cups mushrooms, sliced
- 2 tablespoons olive oil
- 2 cloves garlic, minced
- Salt and pepper to taste
- Fresh parsley, chopped (optional)

Instructions

1. **Heat Oil:** Heat olive oil in a skillet over medium heat.
2. **Cook Mushrooms:** Add mushrooms and sauté for 5-7 minutes until golden brown.
3. **Add Garlic:** Stir in minced garlic, salt, and pepper, and cook for an additional 2 minutes.
4. **Serve:** Garnish with fresh parsley and serve as a flavorful side dish.

Roasted Red Pepper Hummus

Ingredients

- 1 can chickpeas, drained and rinsed
- 1 roasted red pepper
- 2 tablespoons tahini
- 1 tablespoon lemon juice
- 1 clove garlic
- 2 tablespoons olive oil
- Salt and pepper to taste

Instructions

1. **Blend Ingredients:** In a food processor, combine chickpeas, roasted red pepper, tahini, lemon juice, garlic, olive oil, salt, and pepper.
2. **Puree:** Blend until smooth, adding a little water if necessary to achieve the desired consistency.
3. **Serve:** Serve with pita bread or fresh vegetables.

Colcannon (Mashed Potatoes with Cabbage)

Ingredients

- 4 large potatoes, peeled and cubed
- 1/2 small head of cabbage, shredded
- 1/4 cup butter
- 1/4 cup milk or cream
- Salt and pepper to taste

Instructions

1. **Cook Potatoes:** Boil the potatoes in salted water until tender, about 15-20 minutes.
2. **Cook Cabbage:** In a separate pan, sauté the cabbage in butter until soft.
3. **Mash Potatoes:** Drain the potatoes, then mash with butter and milk until smooth.
4. **Combine:** Stir in the cooked cabbage, season with salt and pepper, and serve hot.

Enjoy these delicious side dishes!

Caprese Salad

Ingredients

- 4 ripe tomatoes, sliced
- 8 ounces fresh mozzarella cheese, sliced
- 1/4 cup fresh basil leaves
- 2 tablespoons olive oil
- 1 tablespoon balsamic vinegar
- Salt and pepper to taste

Instructions

1. **Layer Ingredients:** On a serving platter, alternate layers of tomato and mozzarella slices, adding basil leaves between each layer.
2. **Dress Salad:** Drizzle olive oil and balsamic vinegar over the salad, and season with salt and pepper.
3. **Serve:** Serve immediately as a fresh appetizer or side dish.

Grilled Sweet Potatoes

Ingredients

- 2 large sweet potatoes, sliced into rounds
- 2 tablespoons olive oil
- 1 teaspoon paprika
- Salt and pepper to taste

Instructions

1. **Preheat Grill:** Preheat your grill to medium heat.
2. **Prepare Sweet Potatoes:** In a bowl, toss sweet potato slices with olive oil, paprika, salt, and pepper.
3. **Grill:** Place the sweet potatoes on the grill and cook for 6-8 minutes per side, or until tender and grill marks appear.
4. **Serve:** Serve warm as a side dish.

Greek Orzo Salad

Ingredients

- 1 cup orzo pasta, cooked and cooled
- 1/2 cup cherry tomatoes, halved
- 1/2 cucumber, diced
- 1/4 cup Kalamata olives, pitted and sliced
- 1/4 cup feta cheese, crumbled
- 2 tablespoons olive oil
- 1 tablespoon red wine vinegar
- 1 teaspoon dried oregano
- Salt and pepper to taste

Instructions

1. **Combine Ingredients:** In a large bowl, combine cooked orzo, cherry tomatoes, cucumber, olives, and feta cheese.
2. **Make Dressing:** In a small bowl, whisk together olive oil, red wine vinegar, oregano, salt, and pepper.
3. **Toss Salad:** Pour the dressing over the salad and toss to combine. Serve chilled or at room temperature.

Fried Plantains

Ingredients

- 2 ripe plantains, peeled and sliced
- 1/4 cup vegetable oil for frying
- Salt to taste

Instructions

1. **Heat Oil:** In a skillet, heat vegetable oil over medium heat.
2. **Fry Plantains:** Add plantain slices and fry for 2-3 minutes on each side until golden brown.
3. **Drain and Season:** Remove from skillet, drain on paper towels, and sprinkle with salt.
4. **Serve:** Serve warm as a tasty side dish or snack.

Herb-Roasted Root Vegetables

Ingredients

- 2 carrots, peeled and diced
- 2 parsnips, peeled and diced
- 1 sweet potato, peeled and diced
- 1 tablespoon olive oil
- 1 tablespoon fresh rosemary, chopped
- Salt and pepper to taste

Instructions

1. **Preheat Oven:** Preheat your oven to 425°F (220°C) and line a baking sheet with parchment paper.
2. **Toss Vegetables:** In a bowl, toss the diced vegetables with olive oil, rosemary, salt, and pepper.
3. **Roast Vegetables:** Spread the vegetables on the baking sheet and roast for 25-30 minutes, stirring halfway through, until tender and golden.
4. **Serve:** Serve hot as a colorful side dish.

Spinach and Artichoke Dip

Ingredients

- 1 cup frozen spinach, thawed and drained
- 1 cup canned artichoke hearts, chopped
- 1/2 cup cream cheese, softened
- 1/2 cup sour cream
- 1/2 cup mayonnaise
- 1 cup shredded mozzarella cheese
- 1/4 cup grated Parmesan cheese
- 1 clove garlic, minced

Instructions

1. **Preheat Oven:** Preheat your oven to 350°F (175°C).
2. **Mix Ingredients:** In a mixing bowl, combine spinach, artichokes, cream cheese, sour cream, mayonnaise, mozzarella, Parmesan, and garlic. Mix until smooth.
3. **Bake Dip:** Transfer to a baking dish and bake for 25-30 minutes, until bubbly and golden on top.
4. **Serve:** Serve warm with tortilla chips or bread for dipping.

Zesty Lime Cilantro Rice

Ingredients

- 1 cup rice (white or brown)
- 2 cups vegetable broth
- 1/4 cup fresh cilantro, chopped
- Juice and zest of 1 lime
- Salt to taste

Instructions

1. **Cook Rice:** In a saucepan, combine rice and vegetable broth. Bring to a boil, then reduce heat and cover. Cook according to package instructions.
2. **Add Flavor:** Once rice is cooked, fluff with a fork and stir in cilantro, lime juice, lime zest, and salt.
3. **Serve:** Serve as a flavorful side dish with your favorite main course.

Roasted Garlic Mashed Potatoes

Ingredients

- 4 large potatoes, peeled and cubed
- 1 head of garlic, roasted
- 1/4 cup butter
- 1/4 cup milk or cream
- Salt and pepper to taste

Instructions

1. **Boil Potatoes:** Boil the cubed potatoes in salted water until tender, about 15-20 minutes.
2. **Roast Garlic:** While potatoes are cooking, roast garlic by wrapping it in foil and baking at 400°F (200°C) for 30-35 minutes until soft.
3. **Mash Potatoes:** Drain the potatoes, then mash with roasted garlic, butter, and milk until smooth.
4. **Serve:** Season with salt and pepper, and serve warm as a comforting side dish.

Enjoy these delicious side dishes!

Creamed Corn with Bacon

Ingredients

- 4 cups fresh corn kernels (or frozen corn)
- 4 slices bacon, chopped
- 1/2 cup heavy cream
- 2 tablespoons butter
- Salt and pepper to taste
- Chopped chives for garnish (optional)

Instructions

1. **Cook Bacon:** In a large skillet, cook the bacon over medium heat until crispy. Remove and drain on paper towels.
2. **Sauté Corn:** In the same skillet, add butter and corn. Cook for 5-7 minutes until heated through.
3. **Add Cream:** Stir in heavy cream, salt, and pepper. Cook for an additional 2-3 minutes until slightly thickened.
4. **Finish and Serve:** Stir in the bacon, garnish with chives if desired, and serve warm.

Grilled Eggplant with Herbs

Ingredients

- 2 medium eggplants, sliced into rounds
- 3 tablespoons olive oil
- 1 teaspoon salt
- 1 teaspoon pepper
- 2 tablespoons fresh herbs (like thyme or oregano), chopped

Instructions

1. **Preheat Grill:** Preheat the grill to medium-high heat.
2. **Prepare Eggplant:** Brush eggplant slices with olive oil, and season with salt, pepper, and fresh herbs.
3. **Grill Eggplant:** Place on the grill and cook for 4-5 minutes per side until tender and grill marks appear.
4. **Serve:** Serve warm as a flavorful side dish.

Dill Pickle Pasta Salad

Ingredients

- 8 ounces pasta (elbow or rotini)
- 1 cup dill pickles, chopped
- 1/2 cup mayonnaise
- 1 tablespoon pickle juice
- 1 teaspoon Dijon mustard
- 1/4 cup red onion, chopped
- Salt and pepper to taste
- Fresh dill for garnish (optional)

Instructions

1. **Cook Pasta:** Cook the pasta according to package instructions. Drain and let cool.
2. **Combine Ingredients:** In a large bowl, combine the cooled pasta, dill pickles, mayonnaise, pickle juice, Dijon mustard, red onion, salt, and pepper.
3. **Mix and Chill:** Mix until well combined. Refrigerate for at least 30 minutes before serving.
4. **Serve:** Garnish with fresh dill if desired and serve chilled.

Tomato Basil Bruschetta

Ingredients

- 1 baguette, sliced
- 3 cups ripe tomatoes, diced
- 1/4 cup fresh basil, chopped
- 2 tablespoons olive oil
- 1 clove garlic, minced
- Salt and pepper to taste

Instructions

1. **Preheat Oven:** Preheat your oven to 400°F (200°C).
2. **Make Topping:** In a bowl, combine tomatoes, basil, olive oil, garlic, salt, and pepper.
3. **Prepare Bread:** Arrange baguette slices on a baking sheet and toast in the oven for about 5-7 minutes until golden.
4. **Top and Serve:** Spoon the tomato mixture onto the toasted bread and serve immediately.

Smashed Potatoes with Rosemary

Ingredients

- 1 pound baby potatoes
- 2 tablespoons olive oil
- 1 tablespoon fresh rosemary, chopped
- Salt and pepper to taste

Instructions

1. **Boil Potatoes:** Boil the baby potatoes in salted water until fork-tender, about 15-20 minutes.
2. **Smash Potatoes:** Drain and transfer to a baking sheet. Gently smash each potato with the back of a fork.
3. **Season and Roast:** Drizzle with olive oil, sprinkle with rosemary, salt, and pepper. Roast in a preheated oven at 400°F (200°C) for 20-25 minutes until crispy.
4. **Serve:** Serve warm as a delightful side dish.

Sweet Potato Casserole

Ingredients

- 4 cups sweet potatoes, peeled and mashed
- 1/2 cup brown sugar
- 1/4 cup milk
- 1/4 cup butter, softened
- 1 teaspoon vanilla extract
- 1/2 cup mini marshmallows (optional)

Instructions

1. **Preheat Oven:** Preheat your oven to 350°F (175°C).
2. **Combine Ingredients:** In a bowl, mix mashed sweet potatoes, brown sugar, milk, butter, and vanilla until smooth.
3. **Transfer to Dish:** Spread the mixture into a greased casserole dish and top with mini marshmallows if desired.
4. **Bake:** Bake for 30-35 minutes until heated through and marshmallows are golden. Serve warm.

Sesame Green Beans

Ingredients

- 1 pound green beans, trimmed
- 1 tablespoon sesame oil
- 2 tablespoons soy sauce
- 1 tablespoon sesame seeds
- 1 clove garlic, minced

Instructions

1. **Blanch Green Beans:** Bring a pot of water to a boil. Add green beans and blanch for 3-4 minutes until bright green. Drain and cool.
2. **Sauté:** In a skillet, heat sesame oil over medium heat. Add garlic and sauté for 1 minute.
3. **Add Beans:** Add green beans and soy sauce, and stir-fry for 3-4 minutes until heated through.
4. **Finish:** Sprinkle with sesame seeds and serve warm.

Three-Cheese Cauliflower Gratin

Ingredients

- 1 head cauliflower, cut into florets
- 1 cup heavy cream
- 1/2 cup cheddar cheese, shredded
- 1/2 cup Gruyère cheese, shredded
- 1/4 cup Parmesan cheese, grated
- 1 clove garlic, minced
- Salt and pepper to taste

Instructions

1. **Preheat Oven:** Preheat your oven to 375°F (190°C).
2. **Boil Cauliflower:** Boil cauliflower florets in salted water for 5-7 minutes until tender. Drain well.
3. **Make Cheese Sauce:** In a saucepan, combine heavy cream, garlic, salt, and pepper. Stir in cheddar and Gruyère until melted and smooth.
4. **Assemble Gratin:** In a baking dish, combine cauliflower and cheese sauce. Top with Parmesan cheese.
5. **Bake:** Bake for 20-25 minutes until bubbly and golden. Serve hot.

Enjoy these delicious side dishes!

Moroccan-Spiced Carrots

Ingredients

- 1 pound carrots, peeled and sliced
- 2 tablespoons olive oil
- 1 teaspoon cumin
- 1 teaspoon coriander
- 1/2 teaspoon cinnamon
- Salt and pepper to taste
- Chopped parsley for garnish

Instructions

1. **Preheat Oven:** Preheat your oven to 400°F (200°C).
2. **Season Carrots:** In a bowl, toss the carrots with olive oil, cumin, coriander, cinnamon, salt, and pepper.
3. **Roast Carrots:** Spread the seasoned carrots on a baking sheet and roast for 25-30 minutes until tender and caramelized.
4. **Garnish and Serve:** Garnish with chopped parsley and serve warm.

Grilled Polenta Cakes

Ingredients

- 1 cup polenta
- 4 cups water or vegetable broth
- 1/2 cup Parmesan cheese, grated
- 1 tablespoon olive oil
- Salt and pepper to taste

Instructions

1. **Cook Polenta:** In a saucepan, bring water or broth to a boil. Slowly whisk in polenta, reduce heat, and cook for 15-20 minutes until thickened. Stir in Parmesan, salt, and pepper.
2. **Set and Chill:** Spread the polenta into a greased baking dish and let cool in the refrigerator for at least 1 hour until firm.
3. **Slice and Grill:** Cut into rounds and brush with olive oil. Grill over medium heat for 4-5 minutes on each side until golden.
4. **Serve:** Serve warm as a delicious side.

Oven-Baked Parmesan Fries

Ingredients

- 4 large russet potatoes, cut into fries
- 3 tablespoons olive oil
- 1/2 cup grated Parmesan cheese
- 1 teaspoon garlic powder
- Salt and pepper to taste

Instructions

1. **Preheat Oven:** Preheat your oven to 425°F (220°C) and line a baking sheet with parchment paper.
2. **Season Fries:** In a large bowl, toss potato fries with olive oil, Parmesan, garlic powder, salt, and pepper.
3. **Bake Fries:** Spread the fries in a single layer on the baking sheet and bake for 30-35 minutes, flipping halfway, until crispy and golden.
4. **Serve:** Serve hot with your favorite dipping sauce.

Sautéed Swiss Chard with Garlic

Ingredients

- 1 bunch Swiss chard, stems removed and leaves chopped
- 2 tablespoons olive oil
- 3 cloves garlic, minced
- Salt and pepper to taste
- Juice of 1 lemon (optional)

Instructions

1. **Heat Oil:** In a large skillet, heat olive oil over medium heat. Add garlic and sauté for 1 minute until fragrant.
2. **Add Chard:** Add Swiss chard and sauté for 5-7 minutes until wilted and tender.
3. **Season:** Season with salt and pepper. Drizzle with lemon juice if desired, and serve warm.

Roasted Beets with Goat Cheese

Ingredients

- 4 medium beets, peeled and diced
- 2 tablespoons olive oil
- Salt and pepper to taste
- 4 ounces goat cheese, crumbled
- 1 tablespoon balsamic vinegar

Instructions

1. **Preheat Oven:** Preheat your oven to 400°F (200°C).
2. **Season Beets:** Toss diced beets with olive oil, salt, and pepper, then spread them on a baking sheet.
3. **Roast Beets:** Roast for 30-35 minutes until tender, stirring halfway through.
4. **Serve:** Drizzle with balsamic vinegar and top with crumbled goat cheese before serving.

Maple-Glazed Acorn Squash

Ingredients

- 1 acorn squash, halved and seeds removed
- 2 tablespoons maple syrup
- 2 tablespoons butter, melted
- Salt and pepper to taste
- Chopped pecans for garnish (optional)

Instructions

1. **Preheat Oven:** Preheat your oven to 400°F (200°C).
2. **Prepare Squash:** In a bowl, mix maple syrup, melted butter, salt, and pepper. Brush the mixture over the cut sides of the squash.
3. **Roast Squash:** Place squash cut side down on a baking sheet and roast for 30-35 minutes until tender.
4. **Garnish and Serve:** Flip the squash cut side up, garnish with chopped pecans if desired, and serve warm.

Fennel and Apple Slaw

Ingredients

- 1 bulb fennel, thinly sliced
- 1 apple, julienned
- 2 tablespoons lemon juice
- 2 tablespoons olive oil
- Salt and pepper to taste
- 1 tablespoon fresh dill or parsley, chopped (optional)

Instructions

1. **Combine Ingredients:** In a large bowl, combine fennel, apple, lemon juice, olive oil, salt, and pepper.
2. **Toss Slaw:** Toss to coat evenly. Add fresh dill or parsley if desired.
3. **Chill and Serve:** Let the slaw sit for 15-20 minutes before serving to allow flavors to meld.

Tomato Cucumber Salad

Ingredients

- 2 cups cherry tomatoes, halved
- 1 cucumber, diced
- 1/4 red onion, thinly sliced
- 2 tablespoons olive oil
- 1 tablespoon red wine vinegar
- Salt and pepper to taste
- Fresh basil for garnish (optional)

Instructions

1. **Combine Vegetables:** In a large bowl, combine cherry tomatoes, cucumber, and red onion.
2. **Make Dressing:** In a small bowl, whisk together olive oil, red wine vinegar, salt, and pepper.
3. **Toss Salad:** Pour the dressing over the salad and toss to combine. Garnish with fresh basil if desired.
4. **Serve:** Serve chilled as a refreshing side dish.

Enjoy these delicious dishes!

Honey-Lime Roasted Carrots

Ingredients

- 1 pound carrots, peeled and cut into sticks
- 2 tablespoons olive oil
- 2 tablespoons honey
- Juice of 1 lime
- Salt and pepper to taste
- Fresh cilantro for garnish

Instructions

1. **Preheat Oven:** Preheat your oven to 425°F (220°C) and line a baking sheet with parchment paper.
2. **Mix Ingredients:** In a large bowl, whisk together olive oil, honey, lime juice, salt, and pepper. Add carrots and toss to coat.
3. **Roast Carrots:** Spread the carrots on the prepared baking sheet in a single layer. Roast for 25-30 minutes, turning halfway, until tender and caramelized.
4. **Garnish and Serve:** Garnish with fresh cilantro before serving.

Pea and Mint Salad

Ingredients

- 2 cups fresh or frozen peas, thawed
- 1/4 cup fresh mint leaves, chopped
- 2 tablespoons olive oil
- Juice of 1 lemon
- Salt and pepper to taste
- 1/4 cup feta cheese, crumbled (optional)

Instructions

1. **Combine Ingredients:** In a large bowl, combine peas and mint leaves.
2. **Make Dressing:** In a small bowl, whisk together olive oil, lemon juice, salt, and pepper.
3. **Toss Salad:** Pour the dressing over the pea mixture and toss gently to combine. Add feta cheese if desired.
4. **Serve:** Serve chilled as a refreshing side.

Crispy Kale Chips

Ingredients

- 1 bunch kale, washed and dried
- 1 tablespoon olive oil
- Salt to taste
- Optional seasonings: garlic powder, paprika, nutritional yeast

Instructions

1. **Preheat Oven:** Preheat your oven to 350°F (175°C) and line a baking sheet with parchment paper.
2. **Prepare Kale:** Tear kale leaves into bite-sized pieces and place them in a bowl. Drizzle with olive oil and sprinkle with salt and any optional seasonings.
3. **Bake Kale:** Spread the kale in a single layer on the baking sheet. Bake for 10-15 minutes until crispy, checking frequently to prevent burning.
4. **Cool and Serve:** Let cool slightly before serving as a healthy snack.

Wild Mushroom Risotto

Ingredients

- 1 cup Arborio rice
- 4 cups vegetable or chicken broth
- 2 tablespoons olive oil
- 1 onion, finely chopped
- 2 cloves garlic, minced
- 8 ounces wild mushrooms, sliced
- 1/2 cup white wine (optional)
- 1/2 cup Parmesan cheese, grated
- Salt and pepper to taste
- Fresh parsley for garnish

Instructions

1. **Heat Broth:** In a saucepan, bring the broth to a simmer and keep warm.
2. **Sauté Vegetables:** In a large skillet, heat olive oil over medium heat. Add onion and garlic, sautéing until translucent. Add mushrooms and cook until tender.
3. **Add Rice:** Stir in Arborio rice, toasting for 1-2 minutes. If using, pour in white wine and let it absorb.
4. **Cook Risotto:** Gradually add warm broth, one ladle at a time, stirring frequently until absorbed before adding more. This process takes about 18-20 minutes until the rice is creamy and al dente.
5. **Finish Risotto:** Stir in Parmesan cheese, salt, and pepper. Garnish with fresh parsley and serve warm.

Enjoy these delightful recipes!

www.ingramcontent.com/pod-product-compliance
Lightning Source LLC
LaVergne TN
LVHW081503060526
838201LV00056BA/2904